In 1982 Richard Noble was unsuccessful in his attack on the record at Black Rock Desert in Nevada, USA, but despite numerous problems achieved a speed of 590 mph (949 km/h).

C000095111

THE LAND SPEED RECORD

David Tremayne

Shire Publications Ltd

CONTENTS

Copyright © 1991 by David Tremayne. First published 1991. Shire Album 263. ISBN 0 7478 0115 0.
All rights reserved. No part of this publication may be reproduced or transmitted in any form or by any means, electronic or mechanical, including photocopy, recording, or any information storage and retrieval system, without permission in writing from the publishers, Shire Publications Ltd, Cromwell House, Church Street, Princes Risborough, Buckinghamshire HP17 9AJ, UK.

Printed in Great Britain by C. I. Thomas & Sons (Haverfordwest) Ltd, Press Buildings, Merlins Bridge, Haverfordwest, Dyfed SA61 1XF.

British Library Cataloguing in Publication Data: Tremayne, David. The land speed record. 1. Racing cars. Speed records. I. Title. 796.72. ISBN 0-7478-0115-0.

Editorial Consultant: Michael E. Ware, Curator of the National Motor Museum, Beaulieu, Hampshire.

ACKNOWLEDGEMENTS
Photographs are acknowledged as follows: Charles Noble, Project Thrust, cover; Richard Noble, page 31 (bottom); Cyril Posthumus, pages 2, 3, 4 and 5; Project Thrust, page 1. The remaining photographs are from the author's collection.

Cover: *Richard Noble and his Rolls-Royce turbojet-powered 'Thrust 2' blast across the dusty floor of the Black Rock Desert in Nevada on 4th October 1983, the day that he regained the land speed record for Britain at 633.47 mph (1019.44 km/h).*

Below: *The Comte de Chasseloup-Laubat was the first to pioneer primitive streamlining. This pointed nose and tail helped his Jeantaud to 57.6 mph (92.7 km/h) at Achères, France, in March 1899.*

The remarkable 'La Jamais Contente' ('The Never Satisfied') was the electrically powered car in which the Belgian Camille Jenatzy broke the record in April 1900.

FINDING THE POWER SOURCE: 1898 TO 1906

In bald terms, the land speed record is a battle of distance against time, but ever since one man attempted to go faster than his fellows, it has become much more than that. It has come to epitomise courage, daring and initiative, not only of individuals, but of countries. And as man has begun to explore space, it remains one of the greatest challenges that earth can offer. Those who have succeeded in breaking it, and those who have failed or even perished in their attempts, have all been driven by the desire to push a little harder, further and faster, to expand man's knowledge and to tread where no one else has. Record attempts are now expensive undertakings, but as long as the challenge exists there will be, periodically, men who are prepared to take a calculated risk, to venture into the unknown in search of the honour of being the fastest person on earth. But how did it all begin?

In late November 1898 the Automobile Club de France (ACF) sponsored a timed hillclimb at Chanteloup, 20 miles (32 km) from Paris. Rather surprisingly, in view of the infancy of the horseless carriage, no fewer than 54 cars took part, and an electric vehicle driven by Camille Jenatzy from Brussels was declared the winner at 18 mph (29 km/h).

Among those he beat was Comte Gaston de Chasseloup-Laubat in his French-built electric Jeantaud. He secretly requested that the ACF, of which he had been a founder member, stage a *course de vitesse* and it was held over a smooth 1.2 mile (2 km) course in the Achères park at St Germain, near Paris, on 12th December that year.

Jenatzy had a prior engagement, but Chasseloup-Laubat trounced his petrol-engined rivals in the 36 horsepower Jeantaud, whose electric motor drove the rear wheels via chains. It was an exceptionally heavy car, weighing 3205 pounds (1400 kg) with its full complement of batteries, but as the petrol cars spluttered and banged the Jeantaud started off smoothly and the Count was timed at 39.24 mph (63.15 km/h) through the flying kilometre. The land speed record had been established.

Chasseloup-Laubat's success stimulated Jenatzy, the 'Red Devil'. Instantly he issued a challenge, and on 17th January 1899 they met again at Achères. Jenatzy had the first turn and calmly raised the record to 41.42 mph (66.65 km/h), before Chasseloup-Laubat repelled the challenge with 43.69 mph (70.31 km/h).

Ten days later Jenatzy returned alone to Achères to record 49.92 mph (80.33 km/h), and Chasseloup-Laubat's subsequent attempt to retrieve the honours was thwarted initially by mechanical problems and poor weather. Both factors would become regular features of most record attempts.

On 4th March, however, the Jeantaud, now equipped with a sleek pointed nose after much work on its wind-cheating properties, bettered Jenatzy's mark, achieving 57.60 mph (92.69 km/h).

Never one to accept defeat willingly, the 'Red Devil' had been hard at work on the world's first bespoke record contender, a sensational torpedo-shaped projectile that looked like a cigar on wheels. He called it *La Jamais Contente*, 'The Never Satisfied'. With this startling creation he shattered the record on 29th April with 65.79 mph (105.87 km/h), to have the last word in his personal battle with the French nobleman.

Electrical power seemed to be the appropriate means of propulsion as the petrol engine was still at an early stage of development, but the Frenchman Leon Serpollet had other ideas. He worked quietly putting the finishing touches to a steam-powered egg-shaped car, which was aptly called *Oeuf de Pâques*, 'Easter Egg'. On the seafront at Nice during the annual 'Speed Week' on the Promenade des Anglais in 1901 he saw off all the petrol-engined opposition and was little slower than Jenatzy's record. The following year, on 13th April, he steered the Egg down the promenade's kilometre distance in 29.8 seconds, a speed of 75.06 mph (120.79 km/h).

The French Mors was a competitive challenger for the record in the early years of the twentieth century. In July 1902 Baron Pierre de Caters exactly equalled Serpollet's 75.06 mph (120.79 km/h) record. Other Mors drivers went faster still.

The 100 mph (160.93 km/h) barrier was at last broken in 1904, when the Frenchman Louis Rigolly achieved 103.55 mph (166.64 km/h) with this Gobron-Brillié in Ostend, Belgium.

Meanwhile, later in 1902, Mors and Mercedes became the leading marques as drivers used their fine racing cars for record attempts. The American millionaire William K. Vanderbilt was frequently timed as the fastest petrol-engined user, but it was not until 5th August, on a stretch of road at Ablis, that he achieved the record. The Belgian Baron Pierre de Caters had equalled Serpollet's record in July, and now Vanderbilt broke it with 76.08 mph (122.43 km/h).

It was the first of a flood of records. On 5th November Henri Fournier achieved 76.60 mph (123.27 km/h) in a similar Mors at Dourdan, and twelve days later Augières raised that to 77.13 mph (124.12 km/h) in the same car. While the figure had crept up since Serpollet's breakthrough, it then leapt to 83.47 and 84.73 mph (134.32 and 136.35 km/h) in 1903 as Arthur Duray pushed his Gobron-Brillié to the fore at Dourdan.

Complications arose in 1904, the first year in which the Americans took an interest. The conservative ACF, which had timed all previous attempts, refused to accept any American figures as official, since they had not been timed with what it deemed to be 'authorised' equipment. On the frozen Lake St Clair in January 1904 Henry Ford himself drove the crude Ford *Arrow* or '999' to 91.37 mph (147.04 km/h) and Vanderbilt managed 92.30 mph (148.53 km/h) in his Mercedes. He used the sands of Daytona Beach in Florida for the first time, but though they would become a part of record history his new figure was not accepted.

As far as the French were concerned, the next official record was the 94.78 mph (152.52 km/h) set by Louis Rigolly's Gobron at Nice in March. As contenders improved their machines, increases were small and tenancy of the title of Fastest Man on Earth tended to be short.

In May de Caters set a new record at 97.25 mph (156.50 km/h) and the target of 100 mph (160.93 km/h) was at last within reach. Rigolly achieved it first that July with 103.55 mph (166.64 km/h) in his trusty Gobron, only to have the Darracq of Paul Baras steal his laurels months later with 104.52 mph (168.20 km/h). In 1905 Arthur MacDonald reached 104.65 mph (168.41 km/h) with a Napier and Herbert Bowden 109.75 mph (176.62 km/h) with a Mercedes called the *Flying Dutchman*, both on Daytona Beach, but the European authorities refused to recognise the speeds, and instead accepted Victor Héméry's 109.65 mph (176.45 km/h) set with a V8 Darracq in late December.

In 1906 the American Stanley brothers surprised everyone when Fred Marriott drove their red steamer to a sensational 121.57 mph (195.64 km/h) on the sands at Daytona. This was his kilometre figure: through a measured mile he had achieved 127.60 mph (205.34 km/h) but the French refused to accept that. Their vehicle fitted with a new boiler capable of withstanding even greater pressure, the Stanleys tried again in 1907. Marriott's speed was calculated 'in excess of 190 mph (305 km/h)' when the *Rocket* hit a gulley and was smashed along the beach.

Sunbeam's 350 horsepower V12 claimed the record on three occasions. In the form shown it achieved 133.75 mph (215.24 km/h) in 1922, before Malcolm Campbell reached 146 mph (235 km/h) and then 150 mph (241 km/h) with more streamlined bodywork.

Fiat's aero-engined giant 'Mephistopheles', seen here in later years on a trial round perimeter roads at Silverstone, achieved 146.01 mph (234.97 km/h) in July 1924, when driven by Ernest Eldridge.

The showman Barney Oldfield claimed 131.27 mph (211.25 km/h) in this Blitzen Benz at Daytona Beach, Florida, in March 1910, but it was not recognised by the European authorities.

THE BIRTH OF THE SPECIAL: 1906 TO 1927

Although Marriott's Stanley special had been an object lesson, it was some time before other contenders fully learned it. Time and again, expense obliged them to make use of proprietary racing cars to make their attempts, and where Mors, Mercedes and Gobron had hitherto been successful the Benz now took over.

It took three years before the petrol engine caught up with the Stanleys, and at the Brooklands race track in Surrey in November 1909 Victor Hémery finally erased Marriott's record with 125.95 mph (202.69 km/h) in his Benz.

In the following years the colourful American showman Barney Oldfield and his compatriot Bob Burman claimed higher speeds in similar cars but were unrecognised in Europe, and then came an important rule change. From Hornsted's official 124.10 mph (199.71 km/h) set in a Benz at Brooklands in June 1914, shortly before the outbreak of the First World War, all attempts had to be made over runs in opposite directions, to even out discrepancies in course gradient and wind direction. From now on the record would be the average of the elapsed times in each direction. Con-

tenders could still nominate either the kilometre or the mile as the measured distance, but where they achieved both the tendency has always been for the speed over the longer distance to be taken as the official record.

The Americans claimed higher speeds immediately after the war, with Ralph de Palma's 149.87 mph (241.18 km/h) and then Tommy Milton's 156.03 mph (251.09 km/h), but again they were met with scepticism, and it was the British who began to edge closer to the official 150 mph (241 km/h).

The spark-plug magnate Kenelm Lee Guinness achieved 133.75 mph (215.24 km/h) in a 350 horsepower Sunbeam in 1922, and that machine would later provide the first successes for one of record breaking's most doughty exponents, Captain Malcolm Campbell. In the meantime, however, as Campbell concentrated on motor racing, the bespectacled Englishman Ernest Eldridge tussled with the Frenchman René Thomas on a road in Arpajon, France. The Frenchman's vehicle was a twelve-cylinder racing Delage and he was first to set a new record, with 143.31 mph (230.62

km/h) on 6th July 1924. Eldridge used an elderly Fiat racing car, which he christened *Mephistopheles* and into which had been shoehorned a Fiat aero-engine. Thomas unsportingly drew attention to its lack of reverse gear, as required by the regulations at the time, but Eldridge rigged one up and six days later took the record with 146.01 mph (234.97 km/h).

That was the last occasion on which the land speed record was set on a public road. The crude vehicles were achieving speeds few had dared to imagine only a few years before, and now more open speed venues were sought. Later that year, after frustra-

tions at a Danish beach called Fanoe, Campbell took the 350 horsepower Sunbeam, now called *Bluebird*, to the shores of Pendine in Dyfed, Wales. There he narrowly beat Eldridge's record with 146.16 mph (235.21 km/h), one of the smallest increments in history, but returned in 1925 to become the first man to 150 mph with 150.76 (242.61 km/h). His great record career had begun.

It had taken Campbell many months to persuade the Sunbeam boss, Louis Coatalen, to part with the 350 horsepower car, but now that company responded with a new machine, a four-litre V12 racing car driven

Left: *Sunbeam's next contender was the small 4 litre V12, with which Henry Segrave beat Campbell's record with 152.33 mph (245.14 km/h) in 1926. It later raced with distinction.*

Below: *At a time when 180 mph (290 km/h) was considered phenomenal, Segrave's 1000 (actually around 900) horsepower Sunbeam shattered the record when he became the first to exceed 200 mph (321 km/h) at Daytona in March 1927.*

Parry Thomas purchased and modified Count Zborowski's Higham Special and called it 'Babs'. After his death in 1927 it was buried at Pendine, Dyfed, but was subsequently exhumed and rebuilt by Owen Wyn Owen, seen here coping with a carburettor fire.

by another man whose name has become forever associated with the record: Major Henry Segrave. On the sands at Southport, Merseyside, in March 1926 he just passed Campbell's record, with 152.33 mph (245.14 km/h), but another significant development was about to occur.

It was becoming clear that an aero-engined special was the most likely means of breaking the land speed record. John Godfrey Parry Thomas, a quiet Welshman, realised this but was unable to finance construction of his own. Instead, he purchased the Higham Special from the racing driver Count Louis Zborowski and set about adapting it to his needs.

Thomas was a gifted engineer and a fine driver. He worked methodically through the crude machine, which he renamed *Babs*, modifying it where he could afford to. It was powered by an American Liberty V12 engine of 400 horsepower, sufficient for the job, and on 27th April 1926 at Pendine Sands he proved it beyond question. He steered *Babs* up and down the measured course at 169.30 mph (272.45 km/h), but he knew he could go even faster. The following day he did so, raising his own new record to 171.02 mph (275.22 km/h).

Thomas knew that Campbell was preparing an all-new purpose-built *Bluebird* and had heard the rumours that Segrave and Sunbeam were working on a monster car with not one but two aero-engines. His time was short. Through the winter of 1926 he modified *Babs* to improve its streamlining and efficiency and, after Campbell's troubled new car had nudged his own record to 174.88 mph (281.43 km/h) in February 1927, hurried to Pendine just as Segrave's 1000 horsepower Sunbeam was sailing for Daytona.

Thomas felt unwell as he attempted the record on 3rd March but had worked up to 180 mph (289 km/h) when, it was thought, one of the drive chains sheared and decapitated him. He thus became the record's first fatality, and after the giant car had overturned and come to rest it was buried in the sands. Years later it was exhumed by Owen Wyn Owen and restored fully. Further investigation suggested that the chain had not been at fault; rather, a broken wheel was suspected to have pitched *Babs* over, whereupon Thomas sustained his terrible injuries. His death was a shattering blow to Britain, and a reminder that the land speed record was becoming a very deadly game.

Above left and right: *Stung by the British, the Americans fought back valiantly. Frank Lockhart was a mechanical genius who helped to design this beautiful 'Black Hawk' Stutz, but after surviving one accident he was killed in April 1928.*

Below: *The White Triplex, driven by Ray Keech, seen here, broke the record narrowly in 1928, but Lee Bible was killed trying to beat the 'Golden Arrow' s' new mark in 1929.*

Having lost his record to Campbell, Segrave hit back with the sleek 'Golden Arrow'. With minimal fuss he raised the speed to 231.44 mph (372.45 km/h) at Daytona in March 1929. Captain George Eyston inspects it at Goodwood in the 1960s.

BRITISH SUPREMACY: 1927 TO 1947

Thomas's death gave Segrave much cause for concern, for his mighty Sunbeam used chains to transmit the power from its two Matabele aero-engines. He sat between them, one ahead of his cockpit, the other aft, and for the first time in a land speed record contender the bodyshell fully enclosed the wheels.

When he arrived at Daytona the Americans were surprised at the Sunbeam's sleekness, and, with the minimal fuss that always characterised his attempts, the 'Mad Major' confirmed his place in the history books. On his first run a gust of wind blew him off course for agonising moments, and then he had to take to the Atlantic Ocean at the end to cool his overheated brakes, but after a change of Dunlop tyres he slammed back down the sandy course to achieve an amazing average of 203.79 mph (327.95 km/h). Campbell's record had been shat-

tered by the biggest official increase in history!

Campbell himself regarded his rival's achievement with typical sportsmanship and continued the modifications that would find *Bluebird* similar speed. When he went to Daytona in March 1928, however, he found further opposition, this time from the Americans.

Frank Lockhart was a mechanical genius who had had little formal education but could drive a car as well as he could engineer it. After success in dirt and board track racing he surprised the establishment by winning the 1926 Indianapolis 500 mile race at his first attempt. Inspired by a dream of the record, he spent all his savings on the *Black Hawk* Stutz, a beautiful, streamlined, bullet-shaped car powered by two Miller straight-eight racing engines linked to form a supercharged V16 which

11

Henry O'Neal de Hane Segrave was every schoolboy's idea of what a record breaker should be: cool, daring and courageous. His 200 mph (321 km/h) elevated him to hero status on his return to Britain.

produced at least 385 brake horsepower. Calculations suggested a maximum speed potential of 330 mph (531 km/h).

By contrast, Ray Keech's White *Triplex* was a crude tank. It was commissioned by a Philadelphia wire manufacturer, Jim White, and consisted of *three* Liberty V12s in a converted truck chassis, one ahead of the abnormally brave Keech, the other two side by side behind him. There was no clutch and streamlining was restricted to a chisel-shaped nose.

Both new challengers met with mishaps. The Stutz bounced into the sea when caught by a gust of wind, and Lockhart had to be dragged ashore by a human chain. He departed to rebuild his little racer. Then Keech was scalded by a burst water hose. Campbell, meanwhile, broke Segrave's record with 206.95 mph (333.04 km/h) and left for England.

A month later Keech returned, the *Triplex* performing surprisingly well. He became the last American for 35 years to hold the record, with 207.55 mph (334.01 km/h),

but Lockhart's new effort ended in tragedy. He had reached over 200 mph (321 km/h) when a tyre burst and pitched the Stutz over. The engineering genius could not be saved this time, and April 1928 was a black month for the United States despite Keech's success.

As Campbell unsuccessfully tried to break the record at Verneuk Pan in South Africa, Segrave returned to Daytona in 1929 to smash the record with the sleek *Golden Arrow*. Like *Bluebird*, this used a single Napier Lion aero-engine, now with 930 brake horsepower. This time, things went even more smoothly than with the Sunbeam in 1927. The *Golden Arrow*'s working life amounted to a bare 20 miles (32 km) as Segrave sped up and down the beach to average 231.44 mph (372.45 km/h) and regain his record with almost contemptuous ease.

Keech had by now refused to drive the *Triplex*, but it came out to attempt to regain its record in the hands of Lee Bible, who had worked on it in the past. As he lifted off too sharply at the end of a fast run the deceleration threw it into a slide from which he was unable to recover, and he and a photographer were killed. A year later the Englishman Kaye Don failed in his attempt when Sunbeam's final contender, the *Silver Bullet*, proved a total disaster.

It was not until 1931 that Campbell had modified *Bluebird* sufficiently, but then there was no stopping him. At Daytona that year he achieved 246.09 mph (396.03 km/h), closing on 250 mph (402 km/h) in one giant leap. Segrave had been knighted for his *Golden Arrow* record, and now Campbell received the same honour for achieving 4 miles (6.4 km) in a minute. Exactly a year later he duly recorded 253.97 mph (408.71 km/h), *Bluebird* now being equipped with a 1350 horsepower Rolls-Royce power unit.

With Segrave dead, killed on Windermere in June 1930 attacking the water speed record, Campbell had no competition but kept going, determined to reach 300 mph (482 km/h). In 1933 at Daytona he achieved 272.46 mph (438.46 km/h). Two years later, with *Bluebird* completely remodelled to enhance its performance, Campbell was

Above: *Kaye Don's Sunbeam 'Silver Bullet' certainly looked the part, but persistent trouble with its supercharging system led to insuperable problems at Daytona in 1930 and he never bettered 186 mph (299 km/h).*

Right: *With Segrave, Keech and Lockhart dead, Campbell had a clear field, continually modifying the 1927 Bluebird to make it go faster. This is the 246 mph (395 km/h) Napier-engined version from 1931.*

Below: *Not all record cars were sensible. This was the Frenchman René Stapp's rather fanciful interpretation of the genre from 1932. The car was powered by Bristol Jupiter radial engines but was destroyed by fire.*

13

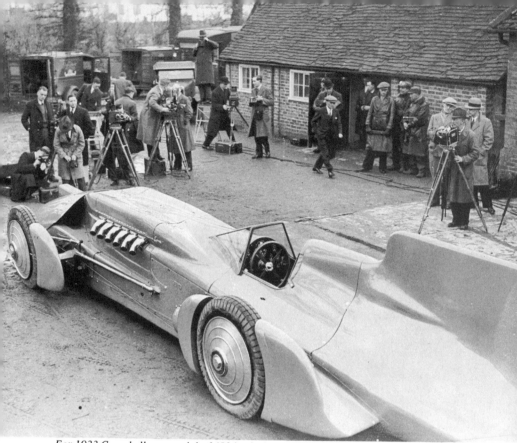

For 1933 Campbell swapped the 1450 brake horsepower Napier Lion engine for the 2300 brake horsepower Rolls-Royce R, and yet again 'Bluebird' raised the record. This time he achieved 272.46 mph (438.46 km/h) on the sands at Daytona.

In 1935 drastic revisions completely changed 'Bluebird's' outline, but despite all the expense wheelspin at Daytona prevented Campbell adding more than 4 mph (6.4 km/h) to his old figure.

Stimulated to find a new site, Campbell took 'Bluebird' to the Bonneville Salt Flats, Utah, later in 1935. There, despite an initial timekeepers' mistake, he succeeded in achieving his aim of breaking 300 mph (483 km/h) on land.

bitterly disappointed to add only another 4 mph (6.4 km/h). The sands of Daytona had yielded all the speed they were going to: Campbell could not get sufficient traction there and began to look elsewhere. He chose the Bonneville Salt Flats, in Utah. On that desolate expanse of brilliant whiteness he finally achieved his ambition on 3rd September 1935, taking *Bluebird* to 301.13 mph (484.60 km/h).

As he then turned his attention, successfully, to the water record, two more Englishmen took up the challenge of the land speed record, both of them, like Campbell and Segrave, successful racing drivers.

Captain George Eyston designed his own *Thunderbolt*, a bulky eight-wheeler with twin Rolls-Royce engines. John Cobb had the esteemed designer Reid Railton draw him a twin Napier Lion-engined teardrop-shaped car, which, with modesty typical of Cobb, they called the Railton Special. Although it used elderly power units, the car was packed with technical ingenuity. Each engine nestled in the curve of an S-shaped backbone chassis, and all four wheels were driven.

Eyston began by breaking Campbell's record with 312.00 mph (502.10 km/h) at Bonneville on 19th November 1937, and

Captain George Eyston designed 'Thunderbolt' himself. It had four wheels at the front for steering and four aft for transmitting the tremendous 4700 brake horsepower from its Rolls-Royce R engines, which were located side by side behind Eyston.

15

In 1937 Eyston broke Campbell's record in the giant 'Thunderbolt'. In its 1938 guise shown here, the twin-engined car attained a new record at 345.5 mph (556.0 km/h).

the following August he raised that to 345.50 mph (556.01 km/h). Then Cobb replied with an easy 350.20 mph (563.57 km/h) in the Railton the first time it ran that September. Eyston further modified his car and accomplished a worthy 357.50 mph (575.32 km/h) a day later, but in August 1939 Cobb had another go. As war threatened, he piloted the Railton to 369.70 mph (594.95 km/h), but even this was not his final achievement.

Cobb returned to Bonneville in 1947, intent on breaking the 400 mph (643 km/h)

barrier. The Railton had been thoroughly rebuilt and, though his average was only 394.20 mph (634.38 km/h), he did reach the 400 in one direction with a speed of 403.13 mph (648.75 km/h). His peak speed was as high as 415 mph (668 km/h).

It was to be the last outright record for piston power and would last longer than any other land speed record. Even today, the record for a piston-engined wheel-driven vehicle is only 6 mph (9.6 km/h) faster, a remarkable tribute to Railton's genius and Cobb's quiet skill.

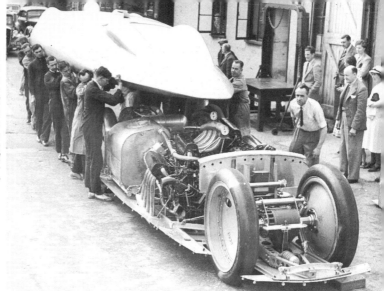

Right: *Sleeker and more scientific than 'Thunderbolt' was John Cobb's car designed by Reid Railton in 1938. It used twin Napier Lion engines beneath a smooth one-piece bodyshell and transmitted its power through all four wheels.*

Left: *In 1938 Cobb broke Eyston's record with 350 mph (563 km/h), regained the record the following year at 369 mph (594 km/h), and eventually averaged 394 mph (634 km/h) in 1947, with a one-way best of 403 mph (648 km/h). Cobb's last record stood officially until 1964.*

JOHN COBB'S
RAILTON SPEED CAR

Right: *In 1949 Cobb demonstrated the tractability of the Railton by running it for exhibition at Silverstone. It is now in the Birmingham Museum of Science and Industry.*

Dr Nathan Ostich's extraordinary 'Flying Caduceus' introduced the jet turbine era at Bonneville during the exciting year of 1960 but had neither the directional stability nor the power to break the record.

A Mormon preacher, Athol Graham, saw his mission to attack the record in a dream. He built his own car, 'City of Salt Lake', but was killed in it at Bonneville during the great confrontation of August 1960.

Donald Campbell's 'Bluebird' CN7 was the pride of British industry and cost a fortune to build. The four-wheel drive, gas turbine-powered projectile was demonstrated at Goodwood before shipment to Bonneville.

INTO THE JET AGE: 1960 TO 1965

As Donald Campbell took up his father's torch and successively broke the water speed record after the Second World War, young Americans developed the 'hot-rod' to the point where the two factions came together at Bonneville in 1960.

By then, Campbell had commissioned the 'car to end all cars', a new *Bluebird* designed by the Norris brothers and driven through all of its four giant wheels by a Bristol Siddeley Proteus gas turbine engine. He had opposition, however. As the size of his team that August amazed the Americans, so he too was amazed when he saw their contenders.

Art Arfons followed accepted practice by cramming an Allison aero-engine into the crude chassis of his *Green Monster Anteater*. Athol Graham used a similar power-plant in his home-built *City of Salt Lake*. Mickey Thompson used a highly scientific approach in his *Challenger 1*, with four Pontiac V8s to drive all four wheels, and Dr Nathan Ostich did with a car what Campbell had done with his *Bluebird* boat

and relied on the pure thrust of the turbojet engine, a technical legacy of the war.

Incredibly, all of them failed. Graham had clocked 344.76 mph (554.82 km/h) the previous December at Bonneville and believed he had nothing more to learn. He accelerated so hard on his first official attempt that he over-strained the rear suspension, which came from a Cadillac road car. When it broke at more than 300 mph (482 km/h) he was killed in the ensuing accident. Arfons withdrew, and Ostich suffered a succession of problems with the jet-powered *Flying Caduceus*.

Thompson, however, came tantalisingly close. A true hot-rodder, he had created an ingenious car in *Challenger*, and when he achieved 406.60 mph (645.34 km/h) in one direction on 9th September the record looked a foregone conclusion. Then, on his mandatory return run, a wheel bearing failed and his chance had gone. He would try again later, both with *Challenger* and the new *Autolite Special*, but stayed unlucky.

Campbell felt even more pressured by

Above left: *While Graham's home-built car was a collection of scrap components, Campbell's was built to aircraft standards, every function of its Proteus engine and associated components being fully monitored.*

Above right: *The hot-rodder Mickey Thompson achieved 406.6 mph (654.3 km/h) in one direction with his ingenious wheel-driven 'Challenger 1' but failed when a wheel bearing broke during his return run.*

Below: *In 1960 'Bluebird', like Graham's 'City of Salt Lake', went too fast too soon and crashed but because of the CN7's structural integrity Campbell escaped with only a fractured skull.*

In 1964 Campbell's 'Bluebird' was rebuilt, with modified cockpit and a tail fin. Despite appalling conditions, he eventually achieved a record of 403.1 mph (648.7 km/h) on the salty Lake Eyre in Australia but by then wheel-driven cars were outclassed.

Thompson's speed. He and Ken Norris initially planned a series of progressively faster runs up to and over record speed. But shortly after *Challenger*'s near success he accelerated too quickly, partly as a result of light-headedness created by a faulty supply of oxygen. *Bluebird*'s wheels spun away their traction, the giant car went sideways at 360 mph (579 km/h) and then flipped and rolled down the course. By a miracle he escaped with only a cracked skull and a pierced eardrum and talked immediately of another attempt.

As Ostich tried again and again in the following years, two new Americans took up the challenge. Glenn Leasher, of San Francisco, drove the jet-propelled *Infinity* for its builder, Romeo Palamides, but like Graham was impatient. He went too fast too soon and died when the silver car rolled over at 250 mph (402 km/h). His accident convinced experts that a tail fin, which *City of Salt Lake*, *Infinity* and the original *Blue-*

bird CN7 all lacked, was an essential part of any record design.

The other American was Craig Breedlove, yet another Californian bred on hot-rodding. He put together his own jet-powered tricycle called *Spirit of America* and in August 1963 achieved a new record of 407.45 mph (655.70 km/h) at Bonneville. The Federation Internationale d'Automobile (FIA), the sport's governing body, at first refused to recognise any jetcar figures since such machines were not driven through their wheels, but after Breedlove's success they relented and set up a new pure thrust category. From that point on, these vehicles would always hold the outright record, and wheel-driven cars operated instead in a class of their own.

Campbell had struggled on vainly, taking *Bluebird* to a salt waste in Australia called Lake Eyre. As his efforts were dogged by continual rain, he realised that the American jets had rendered his expen-

21

The American Craig Breedlove was the first successful pilot of a jetcar. In 1963 he set a 'motorcycle' record of 407.45 mph (655.7 km/h) at Bonneville with this elegant tricycle, 'Spirit of America'.

sive car a white elephant. In an incredibly brave run across an awful course in July 1964 he succeeded in setting the last wheel-driven mark that stood as the official out-right land speed record, but his 403.10 mph (648.70 km/h) was only a little faster than Cobb's one-way best and slower than Breedlove's jet mark. Moreover, the American Tom Green smashed it with 413.20 mph (664.96 km/h) in Walt Arfons's *Wingfoot Express* on 2nd October. An explosion of speed was imminent.

Arfons was then estranged from his brother Art, who only three days later shat-tered Walt's record with his new *Green Monster*, easily reaching 434.02 mph (698.46 km/h). And even that record did not last long. Breedlove returned to Utah with his *Spirit of America* and calmly re-corded 468.72 mph (754.31 km/h) on the 13th October. Convinced he could go faster still, two days later he sped to a sensational 526.28 mph (846.94 km/h). At the end of his run neither of his special braking para-chutes worked properly, and above 200 mph (321 km/h) the disc brakes on his wheels burned out. The *Spirit* careered down the course, sliced through a telegraph

Tom Green was the first man to set an official four-wheel jetcar record, but held it, at 413.20 mph (664.96 km/h), for only three days in October 1964 in Walt Arfons's unusual-looking 'Wingfoot Express'.

Green and Walt Arfons lost their record to Walt's estranged brother Art, who blasted his 'Green Monster' to 434 mph (698 km/h). The record soared as the turbojet took over.

The fresh speeds brought new dangers. After setting a new mark at 526.28 mph (846.94 km/h) in October 1964, Craig Breedlove ended his second run in a brine lake after both of his braking parachutes had failed.

Walt Arfons returned for 1965 with the incredible 'Wingfoot Express', which was powered by solid-fuel rockets. The brave Bob Tatroe reached 476 mph (766 km/h) before fire destroyed the peculiar vehicle.

pole and ended up in a brine lake, from which the fortunate Breedlove emerged unscathed.

Art Arfons had the last word for 1964, with 536.71 mph (863.72 km/h), but the amazing succession of records was not quite finished.

Over that winter Breedlove secretly built a new *Spirit of America*, the *Sonic 1* orig-

inally intended to achieve 750 mph (1206 km/h) and break the sound barrier. In November 1965 he regained his record at 555.48 mph (893.93 km/h), despite another scare when the nose of the car lifted at high speed and the parachute again failed to open.

Arfons swiftly replied with 576.55 mph (927.84 km/h), during which the *Monster* was damaged when one of its Firestone

During the winter of 1964 Breedlove worked on a new 'Spirit of America', the 'Sonic 1'. Like Arfons's 'Green Monster' it was powered by a 15,000 pound (6804 kg) thrust General Electric J79 turbojet and aimed at the sound barrier.

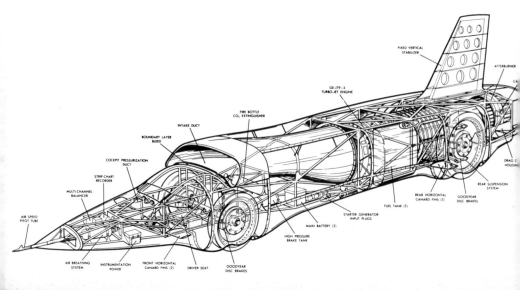

Although 750 mph (1206 km/h) proved too optimistic, Breedlove broke the record twice in 1965 with 'Sonic 1', achieving 555 mph (893 km/h) in early November and then becoming the first to exceed 600 mph (965 km/h) with 600.601 mph (966.547 km/h).

tyres blew out. Breedlove then delighted Firestone's rival Goodyear, which sponsored him, by storming to 600.60 mph (966.54 km/h) a week later.

His tremendous achievement overshadowed another equally worthy piece of history when Bob Summers drove his beautiful quadruple Chrysler V8-powered *Goldenrod* to a new wheel-driven record of 409.27 mph (658.63 km/h) two days earlier, a mark that still stands.

The dangerous game that Arfons and Breedlove were playing was not yet over and in November 1966 Art went over 600 mph (965 km/h) trying to regain his record. A wheel bearing seized and the *Green Monster* broke up down the salt flat. Incredibly, Arfons survived unharmed and in typical fashion discharged himself from hospital only hours later!

After a harrowing accident at 600 mph (965 km/h) in 1966, from which he emerged with only cuts and bruises, Arfons rebuilt the 'Green Monster' for a sound barrier attempt in 1968.

Left: *In 1928, when the record had just passed 200 mph (321 km/h), Fritz von Opel experimented with rocket power in his smooth Opel 'Rak 2' at Avus in Berlin. He achieved 125 mph (201 km/h), but it was still a long time until the day when rockets would challenge for the record.*

Right: *The rocket age began when the Californian Gary Gabelich and the 'Blue Flame' arrived at Bonneville in September 1970. The sleek machine used hydrogen peroxide to produce some 13,000 pounds (5896 kg) of thrust, or 35,000 brake horsepower.*

Left: *In the years after 1970 many American contenders talked of rocket-powered projects. This was Tony Fox's 'Proud American', which existed only in this impressive full-size mock-up form.*

In October 1970 Gabelich, a former trainee astronaut, sped across the salt to average 622.407 mph (1001.639 km/h), breaking Breedlove's 1965 record handsomely.

TOWARDS THE SOUND BARRIER

Almost unnoticed at the height of the Arfons-Breedlove contest of 1965 was another Goodyear-sponsored project, Walt Arfons's rocket-powered *Wingfoot Express*. This used a series of dry-powder JATO (jet assisted take off) rockets. The *Express* was of unusual delta shape and never bettered 475 mph (764 km/h), in the hands of Bob Tatroe, before catching fire when the rockets fired wrongly, but it heralded the era of the rocket engine which the next Goodyear project, the *Blue Flame*, firmly established.

The *Flame* was one of the worthiest of all land speed projects, since for the first time in many years the team behind it, Reaction Dynamics, designed and built not only the chassis but also the rocket motor. This used hydrogen peroxide and was also intended to use liquefied natural gas (LNG) and hydrogen peroxide combined as a bipropellant, and hence it received backing from the American natural gas industry. (In practice, however, the LNG was never used.)

The *Blue Flame* was a pencil-slim projectile 38 feet (11.5 metres) long, with its two front wheels mounted very close together and the rear ones 7 feet (2.1 metres) apart. It was taken to Bonneville in September 1970, with Gary Gabelich, a former National Aeronautics and Space Adminis-

tration astronautical trainee and drag-racer, at the controls. Initial tests revealed a number of teething problems. As they continued, Gabelich had to quell a minor team mutiny created by the loneliness of the inhospitable surroundings, but on 23rd October he at last raised Breedlove's record to 622.41 mph (1001.64 km/h).

As the Californian designer Bill Fredrick began experimenting with his similar but even slimmer *SMI Motivator*, in which the Hollywood stuntman Hal Needham and stuntwoman Kitty O'Neil were said to have surpassed 600 mph (965 km/h), the businessman Richard Noble began work in the early 1970s on Britain's first pure-jet car, a crude device he designed and built himself and called *Thrust 1*.

By 1979 Fredrick's project had spawned the *Budweiser Rocket*, and amid much publicity another stuntman, Stan Barrett, was said to have been timed by the United States Air Force (USAF) at 739.66 mph (1190.03 km/h), or Mach 1.0106, at Edwards Air Force Base in the Mojave Desert. It was the most controversial project in land speed history, with only one run made, over 52.8 feet (16 metres), rather than two over the stipulated kilometre or mile. That was because the *Rocket* could not hold enough fuel for such distances nor be refuelled within the permissible hour be-

Bill Fredrick's 'SMI Motivator' is said to have achieved speeds around 620 mph (997 km/h) at Bonneville in 1976 with Hal Needham, Kitty O'Neil and Simone Boisseree driving. No official records were set.

tween runs. Whatever the team achieved, and it was always clouded by controversy, its mark was not official.

Two years later, in September 1981, Noble and Project Thrust arrived at Bonneville with *Thrust 2*. Designed by John Ackroyd, it measured 27 feet (8.2 metres) long by 8 feet (2.4 metres) wide, resembled the *Green Monster*, on whose concept it was based, and was propelled by 17,000 pounds (7711 kg) of thrust from its Rolls-Royce Avon 302 turbojet. Like both the *SMI Motivator* and the *Budweiser Rocket*, it dispensed with tyres and sat on solid aluminium wheels. That year Noble worked up to an average of 418.19 mph (672.99 km/h) before torrential rain sent his team back home.

In 1982 the salt flats again flooded, but after a very fast relocation to the Black Rock Desert, an alkali playa in northern Nevada, he worked as high as 590.55 mph (950.37 km/h) before the weather closed in again.

In 1979 Richard Noble (left) had progressed his Project Thrust to the point where its Rolls-Royce Avon engine and spaceframe chassis could be joined together. His was the first tangible British project since 1964.

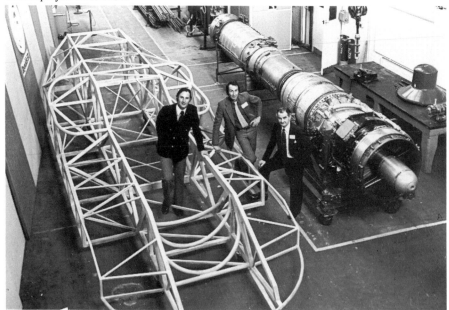

28

With sponsorship for one final try, he returned in 1983. Gradually he worked beyond his 1982 speed, overcoming problems as they developed and surviving one scare when it was feared the engine had been damaged.

Then, on 4th October 1983, Richard Noble finally achieved his nine-year dream. He piloted *Thrust 2* twice across the dusty desert, to an average of 633.47 mph (1019.44 km/h) for the measured mile, to return the land speed record to

Above: *The most controversial project of all was Fredrick's 'Budweiser Rocket', in which Stan Barrett supposedly achieved 739.66 mph (1190.33 km/h) at Edwards Air Force Base, California, in 1979. The timing equipment was not sanctioned by the FIA and the alleged speed was measured for only 52.8 feet (16.09 metres).*

Above: *Throughout 1980 Noble got used to driving 'Thrust 2' in vestigial form on British airfields, setting a series of new British records as a build-up to his attempt at the record.*

Above: *After two years of frustration, Noble eventually succeeded in setting the current record of 633.47 mph (1019.44 km/h) in the Black Rock Desert in Nevada, on 4th October 1983.*

Above: *In 1982 the drag-racer Sammy Miller planned a record attempt with a rocket-propelled tricycle. Despite his experience in rocket cars on British drag strips, however, it never materialised.*

Left: *In 1983 Craig Breedlove assembled this mock-up, intended to raise the necessary sponsorship to produce 'Spirit of America — Sonic 2'. The project remains unfulfilled.*

Below: *A former Project Thrust team member, the American Tom Palm, plans to break the Summers brothers' 409.28 mph (658.65 km/h) wheel-driven record in this turbine-powered streamliner, 'Minnesota'.*

Britain for the first time in nearly twenty years.

After his accident in 1989 when the two-wheeled, lightweight *Green Monster Number 27* rolled over at Bonneville, Art Arfons returned in October 1990, the car now fitted with small outrigged rear wheels. Watched by Noble and his old rival Breedlove, the 64-year-old grandfather, undeterred despite the death of his nephew the previous year in a water-speed record attempt, worked up to a recorded 328 mph (528 km/h) for the measured mile. However, the tiny cockpit filled with salt dust and increasingly serious vibrations were created by the interaction of the metal wheels on the salt. There was also a problem with the afterburner, and finally Arfons decided it was time to retire from record attempts.

Noble's record thus remains intact, but Breedlove has now taken delivery of two fresh General Electric J79s for his latest concept. New challenges will come one day as another adventurer steps forward, his sole aim to become the fastest man on earth.

Above: *Art Arfons, the 'junkyard genius of the jetset', was still experimenting with high-speed projectiles when he crashed his jet-powered bicycle at Bonneville in 1989. Again, he escaped unharmed.*

Below: *Art Arfons could not resist another attempt at Bonneville in 1990, despite a roll at more than 200 mph (322 km/h) the previous year. Serious vibrations finally persuaded him to retire from speed record attempts.*

FURTHER READING

The books listed below are authoritative sources.

Ackroyd, J. *Just for the Record*. C. H. W. Roles and Associates, 1984.

Campbell, Gina (with Michael Meech). *Bluebirds — The Story of the Campbell Dynasty*. Sidgwick and Jackson, 1988.

Kasmann, F. *Weltrekord-fahrzeuge 1898 bis Heute*. Kohlhammer Edition Auto und Verkehr, 1984.

Posthumus, Cyril, and Tremayne, David. *Land Speed Record: From 39.24 to 600+ mph*. Osprey, 1984.

Tremayne, David. *The Fastest Man on Earth: The Inside Story of Richard Noble's Land Speed Record*. 633 Club, 1986.

Tremayne, David. *Automobile Record Breakers*. Quintet, 1990.

Villa, Leo. *The Record Breakers*. Hamlyn, 1969.

Villa, Leo. *Life with the Speed King* (Malcolm Campbell). Marshall Harrison Baldwin, 1979.

PLACES TO VISIT

Intending visitors are advised to find out the times of opening before making a special journey.

Birmingham Museum of Science and Industry, Newhall Street, Birmingham, West Midlands B3 1RZ. Telephone: 021-236 1022. John Cobb's Railton Mobil Special.

Museum of British Road Transport, St Agnes Lane, Hales Street, Coventry, West Midlands CV1 1PN. Telephone: 0203 832425. Permanent display of *Thrust 2* and video film of Richard Noble's land speed record attempt.

National Motor Museum, John Montagu Building, Beaulieu, Brockenhurst, Hampshire SO42 7ZN. Telephone: 0590 612345. Display including 350 horsepower Sunbeam, 1000 horsepower Sunbeam, *Golden Arrow* and *Bluebird* CN7.

Perhaps the most likely to challenge Noble's record is this American rocket car, 'City of Sterling', which is being built by Bill Gaynor of Colorado. He hopes to reach 1000 mph (1609 km/h), but the project has temporarily been abandoned.